D1520981

ROAD TO RECOVERY

# GOLDEN LION TAMARIN

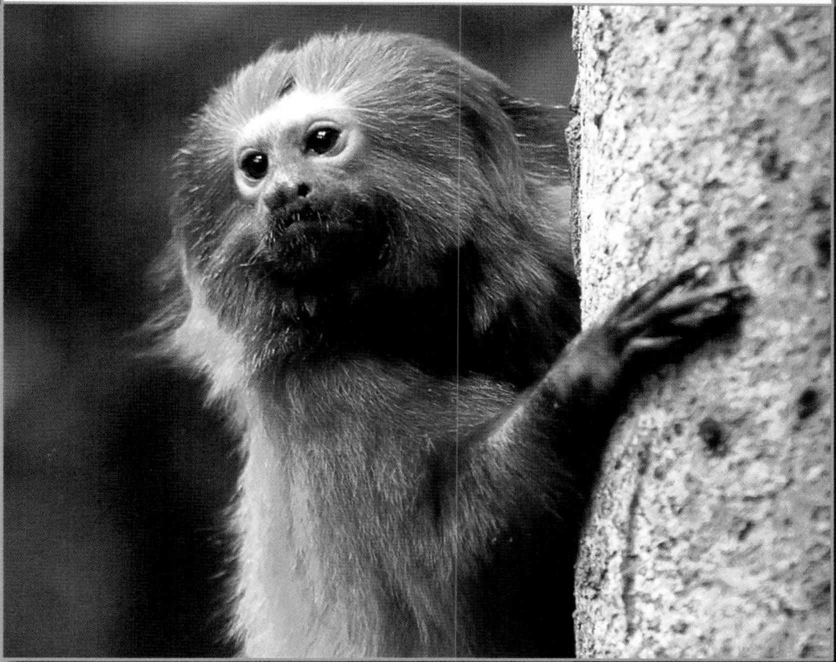

*Barbara A. Somervill*

Cherry Lake Publishing
Ann Arbor, Michigan

Published in the United States of America by Cherry Lake Publishing
Ann Arbor, MI
www.cherrylakepublishing.com

Content Adviser: Devra G. Kleiman, Zoo-Logic, LLC; Senior Scientist Emeritus, Smithsonian National Zoological Park; Adjunct Professor, University of Maryland; Vice-President, Save the Golden Lion Tamarin

Photo Credits: Page 9, Photo courtesy of the Library of Congress; page 26, © Frans Lanting/Corbis; © Philip Marazzi; Papilio/Corbis

Map by XNR Productions, Inc.



Library of Congress Cataloging-in-Publication Data
Somervill, Barbara A.
Golden lion tamarin / by Barbara A. Somervill.
p. cm. — (Road to recovery)
Includes index.
ISBN-13: 978-1-60279-032-2 (hardcover)
ISBN-10: 1-60279-032-9 (hardcover)
1. Golden lion tamarin. I. Title. II. Series.
QL737.P925S66 2007
599.8'4—dc22 2007004446

*Cherry Lake Publishing would like to acknowledge the work of The Partnership for 21st Century Skills. Please visit* www.21stcenturyskills.org *for more information.*

# Table of Contents

CHAPTER ONE

# In Poço das Antas

Dawn shoots the sun's golden rays into the canopy of the Poço das Antas swamp forest in Brazil. In a woodpecker's empty nest, a family of golden lion tamarins wakes after a night's rest. The tamarins peek out of

*The wild golden lion tamarin lives in the state of Rio de Janeiro in Brazil.*

the hollow, carefully checking the surrounding area before emerging. They must be constantly aware of predators.

The tamarins spend their morning hunting for food. Most of the tamarins' diet is fruit, although they also eat nectar, tree sap, and insects as well as birds, lizards, and frogs. This morning, the group is scavenging among bromeliads growing on tree branches high in the swamp forest canopy. The tamarins use their long, thin fingers to dig out insects from between the leaves of the plants and to find water held in the plant.

This family group has six members. The adult male is about six years old, and the female is five. The breeding couple has 14-month-old twins and a second pair not quite two months old.

As the group moves through the trees, the father and the older tamarin juveniles carry the infants. Nursing twins places a heavy demand on the

There are four species of lion tamarins: the golden lion tamarin, the black lion tamarin, the black-faced lion tamarin, and the golden-headed lion tamarin. All four species are found only in the Atlantic rain forests of Brazil. While the golden lion tamarin and the golden-headed lion tamarin are considered endangered, the black lion tamarin and the black-faced lion tamarin are considered critically endangered.

mother, so the rest of the group helps carry, collect food for, and teach the youngest babies.

Tamarins use all four limbs to move from tree to tree. The vines and overhanging branches are like sidewalks to them. They are in a tropical rain forest, thick with tangling vines and trees that form a dense canopy.

The tamarin group stays under leaf cover about 30 feet (9 meters) up in the canopy. Leaf cover hides them from hawks and eagles searching for a meal. The tamarins also need to watch out for boa constrictors, jaguars, jaguarundis, ocelots, and tayras (small weasel-like critters that attack nest holes at night).

The golden lion tamarins stay busy feeding, grooming, and looking out for enemies. A black hawk swoops through the sky, and the tamarins sound a warning and drop low. Tamarins in nearby territories pick up the whine, and soon the swamp forest is quiet. If a snake were detected, however, tamarins would fill the forest with loud repetitive clucks to warn each other of danger.

*A golden lion tamarin raises the alarm to warn others of danger in the forest.*

*Golden lion tamarins spend their days looking out for predators, nibbling on fruit, and moving in the trees above the swamp forest floor.*

Sunset approaches. The group looks for a new nest site for the night. It is safer for them to move around than to stay in a permanent nest.

The group will sleep tucked close together in a tree hole. The infants nurse before sleeping snuggled with their mother. Their older sisters stretch and then cuddle next to each other. The father also curls up nearby. Tomorrow will be another busy day.

CHAPTER TWO

# The Story of Golden Lion Tamarins

In 1521, Portuguese explorer Ferdinand Magellan and his crew first saw lion tamarins. A member of the crew described the animals as "beautiful . . . cats similar to a small lion." Scientists now know that the bright orange golden lion tamarin is neither a cat nor a lion. It is a New World monkey, a member of the family that includes marmosets, capuchins, and squirrel monkeys.

*Two other species that Magellan discovered on his voyage around the world were the llama and the penguin.*

*An important physical feature of the lion tamarin is its long hands, which it uses to find insects.*

Among New World monkeys, lion tamarins are unusual because they do not have **prehensile** tails. Other New World monkeys use prehensile tails to hang from vines and branches. On the other hand, tamarins are similar to other monkeys because they are diurnal. They hunt for food by day and sleep at night.

Lion tamarins have very long hands with slender fingers and clawlike fingernails. The length of their fingers equals the length of their forearms. These slim fingers dig into small holes in trees or plants. There tamarins find insects of all sizes to eat.

Their normal food, however, is fruit—and lots of it. The sugar content of fruit, nectar, or plant sap gives tamarins the energy needed to keep warm and healthy.

Some scientists believe golden lion tamarins get their remarkable color from sunlight. Can you think of ways that the sun affects other animals?

Golden lion tamarins are small monkeys, about the size of a squirrel. They measure 12 inches (30 centimeters) tall. The tail stretches another 13 to 17 inches (33 to 43 cm). Their bodies are covered with bright orange-gold, carrot-colored fur several inches thick. Golden lion tamarins have

*In spite of having several inches of colored fur, the skin of the golden lion tamarin can still get exposure to the sun.*

a mane of hair around their head, like a lion. They weigh between 21 and 25 ounces (about 600 and 700 grams), with males weighing slightly more than females.

Females are able to reproduce at about 18 months old. Pregnant females carry their babies for 125 to 132 days before giving birth. They may have one or two litters a year, and nearly 80 percent of wild golden tamarin litters produce twins. Captive lion tamarins may have triplets and even quadruplets. The pregnant female only weighs about 1.7 pounds (771 g). At birth, a golden lion tamarin infant sometimes weighs only 2.5 ounces (71 g).

Although 90 percent of golden lion tamarin babies survive to about three months old, 25 percent die or disappear during the first year of life. Why do you think so many young tamarins fail to reach adulthood?

Mothers nurse their infants every two to three hours for about three months. The babies grow rapidly. After the first 10 days or so, the father and older siblings take over carrying the infants. This training helps prepare the juveniles for parenthood. Besides, the mother needs to save her energy for nursing her youngsters.

*This golden lion tamarin baby travels on the back of its father or an older brother or sister.*

When lion tamarins reach adulthood at about 18 months, they may leave the family group to find mates of their own. This process is called dispersal.

Females tend to leave first. During a female's travels, she looks for a single male of mating age or a group that needs an adult breeding female. About 75 percent of adult females meet single males, and the rest join established groups. Males, on the other hand, may stay in their family group and can inherit territories.

In the wild, most golden lion tamarins live only 8 to 15 years. Captive lion tamarins may live longer. Tamarins in zoos are fed daily and have no predators to worry about. Zoo life is much safer for a golden lion tamarin than life in the wild. Yet tamarins—like other wild creatures—belong in their native habitat.

CHAPTER THREE

# Endangered!

There probably were never millions of golden lion tamarins swinging through the Atlantic rain forests of Brazil. But there may have been many thousands.

*The golden lion tamarin's remaining habitat is made up of patches of forest separated by deforested areas. This separation makes it harder for the population to grow.*

By 1970, however, it was obvious that the golden lion tamarin population was dwindling. Estimates suggested that their numbers were barely 200. The golden lion tamarin was not simply endangered. Tamarins had become incredibly rare, and their status was critical.

The golden lion tamarin was not the only monkey species in trouble. Thirty-two species of small monkeys—marmosets, squirrel monkeys, and tamarins—lived in the Brazilian rain forests. These small monkeys were all losing their habitats. People cut down millions of trees for timber and built roads through the rain forests. Once the trees were gone, clearing the land for farms, homes, highways, and cities and towns was easy.

Unfortunately for golden lion tamarins, the area in which they had thrived was one of the most populated regions of Brazil. It was almost a suburb of the city of Rio de Janeiro.

The International Union for the Conservation of Nature and Natural Resources (IUCN) is a nongovernmental organization that compiles information about endangered species. Although its headquarters is in Switzerland, it brings together 83 nations, hundreds of organizations, and 10,000 experts worldwide. The IUCN is very influential because of its wide collaboration with scientists, government officials, and business leaders.

One important job of the IUCN is to determine the degree to which a species is at risk of extinction. They label a species "critically endangered," "endangered," or "vulnerable."

In 2003, the IUCN changed the status of golden lion tamarins from "critically endangered" to simply "endangered." Though the species is still in trouble, it has taken a step in the right direction.

As the human population exploded, more than 90 percent of the Atlantic Forest, a tropical swamp forest along the eastern coast of Brazil, disappeared. In the specific area where golden lion tamarins currently live, 98 percent of their original forest is gone.

In addition to loss of habitat, hunting and collecting also reduced the wild tamarin population. In the 1960s and 1970s, hunters captured lion tamarins to sell to zoos, laboratories, and pet stores. This practice was legal at the time, and many animals ended up in medical laboratories. Monkeys serve as lab animals because their genetic structure is similar to that of humans.

It took hard work and some luck to bring golden lion tamarins back from the brink of extinction. Interested groups set up the Golden Lion Tamarin International Research and Management Committee. Zoos worldwide joined to fight for the golden lion tamarins' survival. It was a battle that conservationists could not afford to lose.

Golden lion tamarins play a role in nature just like any other animal. As they feed on fruit, they swallow seeds. When the tamarins pass solid waste, many undigested seeds survive. The waste falls to the forest floor and fertilizes the soil. The seeds in the waste are spread throughout the tamarins' territory, allowing new plants to grow on the forest floor.

Tamarins also affect the insect population. A tamarin family carefully moves through its territory in search of food. As the tamarins hunt, they reduce the number of insects in the rain forest.

In turn, larger predators such as eagles, hawks, jaguars, jaguarundis, ocelots, tayras, and snakes feed on tamarins. But they do not eat everything—leftovers provide food for smaller birds, rodents, and countless insects. This is all part of nature's cycle.

Humans, too, are a part of nature's cycle. Think of what you eat, use, and throw away. How do you affect your environment and the other creatures in it?

CHAPTER FOUR

# The Road to Recovery

Recovery for the golden lion tamarin depended on an international research and management plan. This plan mapped out goals and activities

*The Brazilian government listed the golden lion tamarin as an endangered species in 1968. This action gives a species the highest degree of legal protection.*

needed to ensure that the species thrived and recovered. Every endangered species needs a similar program of clear goals and objectives.

The golden lion tamarin project began with the goal of securing and protecting the current population in the wild. Then in 1972, a captive breeding program started with tamarins in zoos. Zoo-raised animals needed to learn survival skills for the wild. How would they find food? Could they avoid being eaten by the first predator that came along?

The captive breeding program involved zoos worldwide. Participating zoos maintained tamarins in family groups, just like tamarins in the wild. As young tamarins became adults, they were shipped off to new zoos, where they met mates and founded new family groups. This plan copied dispersal, the way tamarins normally form new groups in the wild.

At the same time, studies examined how golden lion tamarins lived in the wild. The program monitored animals reintroduced near Poço das Antas to determine how they were adapting to the wild. The swamp forest also needed protection from further habitat loss.

As captive populations increased, plans were created to reintroduce even more animals into their natural habitats. Family groups at key zoos

*Two golden lion tamarins feed on fruit at a zoo. Zoo-raised animals must learn how to survive in the wild if they are to be released.*

began training in free-ranging zoo habitats where the tamarins could roam. The tamarins no longer got food without having to work to find it. Zoo workers hid oranges, bananas, and other fruits in nooks. They stuffed mealworms and crickets into holes in tubes. Places that held food changed daily, just as they would in the wild.

If reintroduction was to succeed, golden lion tamarins needed more space and a safer environment. In addition to reintroducing captive golden lion tamarins into the wild, conservationists **translocated** some threatened families into a safe habitat in Brazil's protected União **reserve** in 1994. To translocate means to move wild populations to new habitats.

Another key element to making the golden lion tamarin project a success was public education. Most Brazilians knew nothing about tamarins 30 years ago. Conservationists worked to teach the public about

With the combined efforts of the Brazilian government and the zoos that collaborated in the captive breeding program, lion tamarin populations are improving, but there is still a long way to go. As of 2005, the golden lion tamarin population was estimated to be more than 1,200, the black lion tamarin population to be more than 1,000, the black-faced tamarin population to be 400, and the golden-headed lion tamarin population to be between 6,000 and 15,000.

these animals through television programs, school lessons, and tourist events.

Thanks to conservationists' efforts, the golden lion tamarin went from being an unknown species to the most popular animal in Brazil. Golden lion tamarins appeared on stamps, T-shirts, and paper money. They became a symbol for saving the rain forest.

CHAPTER FIVE

# Golden Lion Tamarins Today

In 2001, the 1,000th golden lion tamarin in the wild was born. In just more than 30 years, a rare and critically endangered species had reached a major milestone.

More than 30 percent of those 1,000 wild tamarins trace their existence back to animals that were reintroduced through the captive breeding program. The golden lion tamarin conservation program is well on its way to meeting its

*A golden lion tamarin carrying a baby screams from a tree branch.*

*A forester plants a seedling for a reforestation project near Poço das Antas Reserve in Brazil.*

goal of 2,000 animals in the wild by 2025.

The Brazilian government played a major role by establishing protected rain forests for the golden lion tamarins. Poço das Antas and União Biological Reserve provide homes for the current wild populations.

A number of local families have also created mixed farm/forest land programs that provide habitats for tamarins and profitable crops for people. Several conservation groups provided the education and money necessary to start these mixed farms.

Efforts to regrow rain forest **corridors** will also help. They will provide links between small sections of rain forest where tamarins live and new habitats.

Since 1984, 153 golden lion tamarins have been reintroduced from zoos into the wild. Many survived and produced more young. In 2000, reintroductions stopped due to a lack of available land. The next year, 85 births took place in the wild. Those births are directly linked to reintroduced tamarins. The captive breeding program continues so that a population of animals is always ready to join the wild.

The National Zoo in Washington, D.C., has a program for citizens to help save the golden lion tamarins. It is called Adopt-a-Golden Lion Tamarin. When you adopt a zoo animal, it stays at the zoo, but you pay a small fee that allows staff to provide food, medical care, research, and habitat improvements for endangered species. Most zoos have similar programs, and many schools across North America have made adopting a species part of their environmental education programs.

This is one way individuals can take responsibility for a big problem. Ask your teacher or search the Internet for other ideas on how you can help save endangered species.

After translocation began in União in 1994, conservationists had moved a total of 43 tamarins in 6 family groups by 1997. Within six years, the population had expanded to 120 tamarins living in 16 groups. Both males and females born in União have produced healthy young.

Golden lion tamarins teetered on the brink of extinction 30 years ago. Today, they are a **flagship** species of the conservation movement. If they are saved, then the Atlantic Forest will also be saved.

*Two golden lion tamarins huddle together on the branch of a tree.*

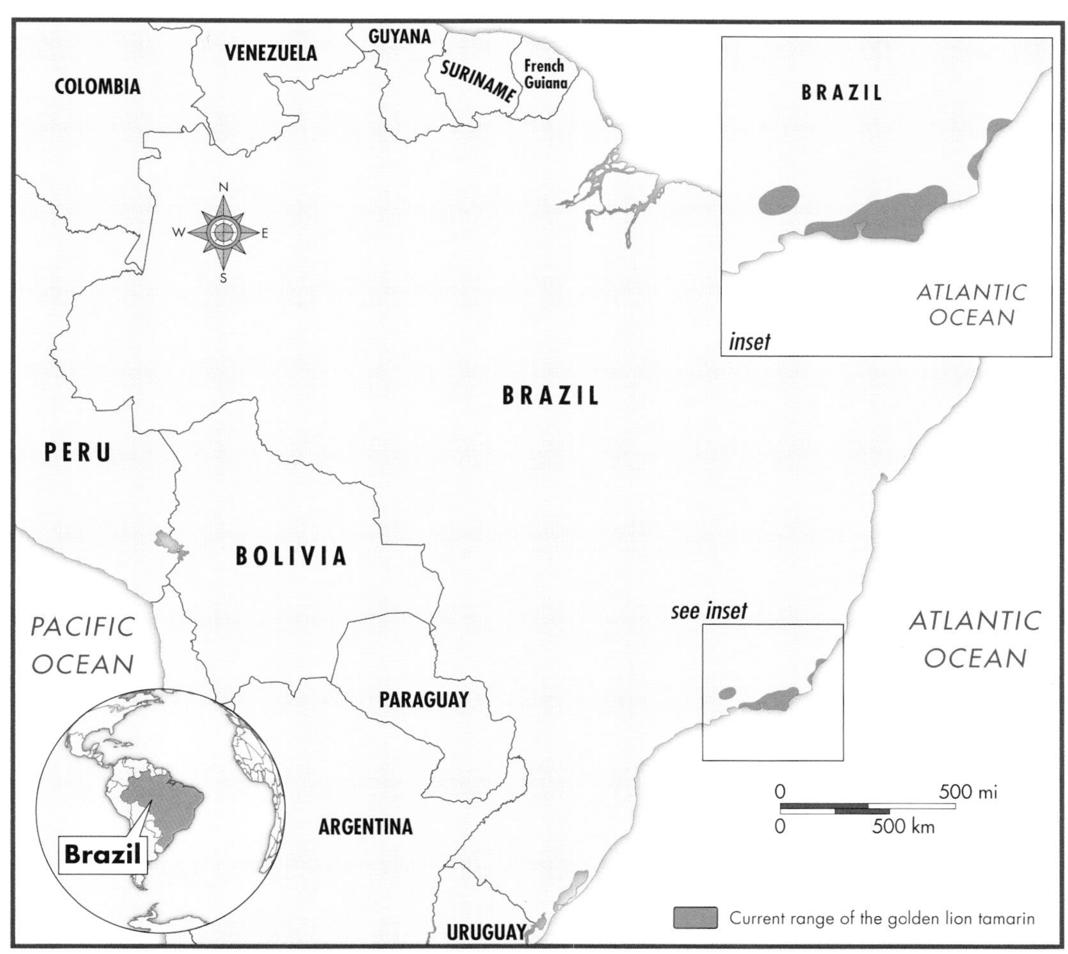


*The current range of the golden lion tamarin, shown in this map, has been much reduced over the past 100 years. The greatest threat to the tamarins' survival is habitat loss.*

# Glossary

**bromeliads (bro-MEE-lee-adz)** tropical plants with fleshy leaves that form a funnel that holds water

**canopy (KAN-uh-pee)** the uppermost layer of plant life in a rain forest

**conservationists (kon-sur-VAY-shun-ists)** people who work to preserve environments, animals, and plants

**corridors (KOR-u-dorz)** connections between habitats

**dispersal (diss-PUR-suhl)** the movement of an animal away from its family unit

**diurnal (dy-UR-nuhl)** more active during the day and more restful at night

**extinction (ek-STINGT-shun)** the condition of no longer existing

**flagship (FLAG-ship)** the best of its kind, used as an example for others

**genetic (jih-NEH-tik)** involving the characteristics passed from parents to their young through genes

**predators (PREH-duh-terz)** animals that hunt and eat other animals

**prehensile (pre-HEN-suhl)** adapted to wrap around something or take hold of it

**reserve (ree-ZURV)** a place set aside for the protection of animals

**species (SPEE-sheez)** a group of similar animals or plants

**swamp forest (SWAHMP FOR-ist)** rain forest that floods for part of the year

**translocate (trans-LOH-kate)** to move wild populations to new habitats

# For More Information

## Books


Ancona, George. *The Golden Lion Tamarin Comes Home.* New York: Macmillan, 1994.

Donald, Rhonda Lucas. *Endangered Animals.* Danbury, CT: Children's Press, 2001.

Jackson, Tom. *Nature Fact File: Monkeys.* London: Southwater, 2005.

Martin, Patricia A. Fink. *Monkeys of Central and South America.* Danbury, CT: Children's Press, 2000.


## Web Sites

The Golden Lion Tamarin Association
*www.micoleao.org.br*
For the Web site of the Golden Lion Tamarin Association, outlining their history and mission

National Zoo: FONZ—Golden Lion Tamarin Conservation Program
*nationalzoo.si.edu/ConservationAndScience/EndangeredSpecies/GLTProgram/*
For information on the conservation program at the National Zoo

The Wild Ones: Lion Tamarins
*www.thewildones.org/Animals/tamarin.html*
To find a profile of lion tamarins that includes photos

# Index



# About the Author

**Barbara A. Somervill** writes children's nonfiction books on a variety of topics. She is particularly interested in nature and foreign countries. Somervill believes that researching new and different topics makes writing every book an adventure. When she is not writing, Somervill is an avid reader and plays bridge.